AVOIDING REGRETS
Quotes of empowerment

By Darryl Taylor Kravitz

Life is the canvas.
We are but paints mixed on the
palette of time.

Darryl Taylor Kravitz

Dedication

For Scott J Roy who will always be my brother in my heart. He was one of the few that made the canvas we were mixed on that much brighter.

Thanks

My undying gratitude goes to my wonderful wife Malika for she filled the void in my heart to succeed. All the dynamics of all the creative pursuits, years ago and in the years to come are the byproduct of her love in my heart.

Creativity is finding a new path on an old road.

Introduction

Artists, Writers & Musicians in order to embrace the beauty of that creative insight, are isolated for a good part of their life to develop their craft. The compilation of these quotes from my mind's heart I cannot take credit for. I feel they were divinely inspired not for self gratification but for universal insight. For example, a dandelion is brighter than the green lawn. It's yellow petals and its vibrant color appears for a time but what happens to a dandelion? It dies quickly of the flower to a white orb of seeds that are carried by the wind to grow more dandelions. So is art, so is writing, so is music and so is life. For certain people will share information and those messages will impact our life. The reason that I wrote this book of quotes is because I believe there is a responsibility in insight for others. So as a dandelion, so my prayer, my heart is that these quotes will help others to avoid the certain pit falls in life that many have endured that I myself have fallen into in a season. It is for the betterment of mankind and I pray that the words written as you read them will give you enlightenment to avoid regrets. - Darryl Taylor Kravitz

Believe! Perceive! Achieve!

Regrets

To reflect too much on what could have been

Leaves no room for what can be.

Faith

Never think you can be more than you believe

Dream more to become more

For if the ladder is short

The journey is even shorter.

Regret

Revisit a time of pain in your life to learn from it

It is less painful in reflection

And a lesson you do not want to repeat

Forward steps

Always look forward to better yourself

Having a direction and a chosen path

For if you look back too much

You won't see the bumps in the road and fall flat on your face

Vision

Never regret what can not change

But be wiser in things you can

Wisdom

If you carry someone else's shoes upon your back

You carry the weight of someone else's misfortune

This slows your journey making it harder to walk forward

Love

Don't ever think love will never come into your life

For it may already be there and you have closed your eyes to it

Sometimes when you see you need to really look

Wisdom

Always fall in love with what you will do next

You will find more desire to complete the current task

And reflect back in a season of what you have achieved

Wisdom

Begin at the end of a goal and work backwards to where

you are now

To see how it is possible

Wisdom

Never change what people admire

Move to change what they don't desire in you

Use what you have done before

To find strength to become more

Life

It is finding a new path to make you smile

Hope

Never walk in the dark without holding a light

Be it above, in your hand, or in your heart

Success

Never be envious of someone else's fortune

Focusing on them takes away the focus on yourself to earn

your own success

Learn from their example

For if they had envy they never would have found their

fortune

Interaction

Compliment people with a true heart

Never a clouded intention

For they will see through your sincerity as muddy water

If it is not sincere say nothing

Wisdom

Always go out of your way to help people

Begin with moving a single stone

Before you commit to moving a whole wall

For if they take advantage

It is easy to drop one stone

Then the commitment of your word to move more

Love

Do not see love as the weakest emotion but the strongest

For through love of discovery or in the heart

So where the accomplishments of man born

Wisdom

Never plan to fail

Never plan to lose

Always plan a strategy to win

Avoid those who have already lost

Life

Always give back to the pool

Of your knowledge, of your strength, of your care

For others to drink from your experience

Warning

Walk with your head held high

But never too high to the point of arrogance

For as looking down in failure you will also fall

Warning

To achieve true wealth in coins or heart

You must weigh the measure of what it takes

And what it will take away from you if you are not careful

Hope

Never be afraid of love

Never be afraid of failure

Never be afraid of success

Never be afraid or plant fear in your heart

For you will have already failed

Till you pull out the weed with faith

Wisdom

The mind will control the heart

Or the heart will control the mind

Remember you are in control of which controls which

Joy

A smile will always go further then a frown

They both begin inside

And the choice begins in the same place

For if you smile inside it will shine forth to your face

Happiness

Laughter will always wash away the tears of sorrow

It is a mindset before the first rain cloud forms

to wash away your joy

Joy

Find something funny and replay it over and over

If it makes you laugh

It can change your disposition

Warning

Never let emotions bottle up

For the pressure will increase

And will always come out at the wrong time and for the

wrong end

Forgiveness

Do this when you don't want to

This is the stepping stone to a brighter path

And a stronger bridge to the future

Forgiveness

To say you cannot forgive

Is to say your heart is afraid to grow

Life

Frustration is part of life

What you do with it

Determines what kind of life you will have

Life

Sometimes learning is to acknowledge

what you should unlearn to learn again

Success

Make a goal to see the reflection of a successful you

in the mirror each day

Till it becomes the true reflection

Wisdom

Sometimes when the sky is darkest in life

Is the knowledge of knowing that when the clouds depart

We appreciate the light that much more

Warning

If you live to hurt others

You will be throwing a boomer rang at your own head

And die in despair

Truth

Failure is only a prison if you look at the bars

For failure is never a prison it is a lesson

To soar above

For you have learned what not to do

Life

To be obsessed with anything

Leaves no time to enjoy the other pastels of life

A rainbow of one color mutes the other things that make life

worth living

Success

Plan the path before you make the journey

Anticipate the obstacles before you hit them

Or they will hit you

Stalling your stride to your dreams

Warning

Never run before you can walk

Never walk before you can crawl

In any pursuit begin with a step of faith

And a desire to run

Success

Wealth has many coins

Yet different currencies

See the riches in a sincere smile

And an open heart as priceless

Wealth

To value greed

Is to be poor in virtue

Penniless in old age

Hope

Never whisper in faith

But shout in its actions

Wisdom

Comb the past out of your mind

Better to have a full head of accomplishments

Then a brush full of long forgotten sorrow

Hope

To contemplate too much on a road

Leaves no room for faith

And no path that you have started to walk on

Learning

Give back more then lip

If you speak too much and not seek to listen

It will make the your words hollow

Balance the tongue

Or the ears will turn to deafness.

Warning

Regret is a key to new wisdom

to finally learn what not to do again and not repeat.

Warning

You can't let hurt plant seeds

These weeds will choke the heart

And strangle the need to love

Hate

You should never plant the seeds of hate

For they bring new gardens of a cursed harvest

Warning

Get out of the rainfall of reoccurring tears.

Emotions

They can be the anchor that you are not aware of

Without wisdom as the sail

And the past to the aft

It leaves the boat stuck in the port

Faith

Denial is a nightmare

Hope is a daydream

And faith is the answer to wake up

Life

To become as a child again

Allows you to relive the beauty of a spectrum that never

becomes dull

For in the eyes of youth, love and hate are not seen in the

other colors of life

Learn to play, smile, and not ever see the dark hues of fear

For we are taught to focus on them through life

Our heart can see the beauty around us at any age by turning

on the mind's light to a rainbow of joy

Life

Making excuses for past things you have done

Leaves no future for changing for the better

Truth

Your emotions are as a chalkboard that other people read

defining you

You can decide what to write but first erase the fear and anger.

Try using a different color chalk and calmer actions

Truth

The beauty in life is not in the striving to the dream.

It is when you do succeed to inspire other people along the

way.

Truth

Your actions are the definition of your heart

Wisdom

Faith will move mountains

But lack of faith will form mountain ranges

Confidence

Keep the glow of day light in your heart even when

the storms of life come crashing down.

Wearing your sunshine inside

keeps you aware that all storms will eventually pass.

Hope

Man avoids the things he fears

It is the very thing that will open the lock of indecision

through a confident action in faith.

The key is inside

The lock I already mentioned

Truth

If you count the stars you will never

have time to enjoy the sky

Warning

Dance and laugh but never at the expense of others.

Love

The fortress of mud and straw protecting the heart

will melt in the rain of tears to say I'm sorry.

Warning

The mirror of your life is a chosen reflection

or a distraction brought about from others

that taught you how to look at the image in the glass

You can choose the you that you want to see

Warning

Who we are will never be more important

as who we strive to be.

Truth

To circum to lying is to be as a flower grown by deception

Watered by deceit, and nurtured by the soil of denial

till it plants the thorns that choke truth and your heart

Warning

Don't give yourself permission to fail

Truth

True Love is the sweetest nectar that is elation in its sip

and life changing in its gulp.

Truth

The greatest thing you can teach your children

is not to learn your own mistakes.

Envy

The garden grows when those of petal are able to water

the new seeds

With wisdom not jealousy. Never be envious that their

flowers may be brighter some in fact will be.

Warning

Immaturity is making excuses for

the mistakes you are going to make

Truth

The only magic the past has over you is what you

Allow yourself to believe

As with magic it is just a trick

Warning

Our tongues wield the blade when this sword

is of harsh words to bury the purpose

in jabbing, poison, dipped steel

looking to draw blood

To hurt others with words

We are stabbing our own self in the heart

Truth

The end result of man's quest to greatness is in learning

from others' actions

And then learning what we need to change to be like them

Truth

It is often said you can not see the forest through the trees

Dreamers know they are in the forest and look to the skies

Truth

How many whispers of justice can turn into a voice?

Depending on the hearts that sing out in a unified purpose.

Warning

An idea will die if you let another crush

You vision with their mallet of lack of insight

Truth

Inspiration can be many demons

They tend to travel in groups.

Better to focus on one idea to convert to angel's wings.

Warning

Let the travel less travelers have their mental journeys

Don't hold their bags or you will never leave on your purpose.

Many have shared a workless dream to leave them stuck on

the dock

Warning

Fools waste time by wasting action on wasting time

Fear

To stand still in a purpose means you have none

Regret

Some things are worth more in memory then in regret

Regret leaves no room for the future

for it feeds on the failures of the past.

Truth

When the obstacle is more important then the goal,

The fear is stronger then the dream

Warning

When you climb through failures you have

carved your footsteps to better understanding.

When you repeat the same steps

you haven't even begun to climb at all

Truth

A candle of faith is brighter then an inferno of hope

Warnings

The rust starts when neglect of metal begins

Such are true in relationships and love

Truth

When we build bridges of hate

we are destine to drown in the river

Truth

Believe in being more then

your worst memory of failure

Warning

To be a leader you need to follow other leaders to learn

If not you are destine to follow only regrets, defeat

and the backs of other soldiers

Truth

Look beyond the present and use the past as a ladder

that only goes in one direction

up

Truth

To carve a dream one must chisel the stone with the right tools

Finding those tools is the start of the design

Learn

Children are always a blessing they are only

a curse by not teaching them enough

Warning

To plan evil is to close the coffin lid

on love and yourself

Truth

Never run where you are afraid to step

Truth

Give more then you take

and take even less in measure to the wealth you give

This is true in coin, heart and time

Warnings

If you don't count your blessings

you will repeat your curses

Faith

Hope is a thin branch

Faith is a stronger limb

Warning

Commit to a journey and not let the grains of sand

that are caught under your foot seem as boulders.

If you believe it they will become them.

Warning

Imaginary tigers claw as painful as real ones do

Giving

Give out of a joyous hand

for a bitter hand infects the harvest

to bitter seeds choking future generosities.

Warning

Chase the words of knowledge with the hunger

of a man in the desert. For true hunger is feed in wisdom

Warning

To deceive is to lie to your own heart til it believes

Warning

The arrogance in science and math is to leave God

out of the equation and add pride in the process.

Love

We choke the seed of love with anger and deny

the garden that could have been with harsh words.

Warning

Evil throws boomerangs at itself and cries why me?

Warning

To walk away from a blessing starts with lack of faith

and begins with lack of vision.

Hope

The truth's of faith are choked by emotional vines

that take the breath from dreams by stalling action.

Joy

The greatest surprise in life is to find out the impact of lives

changed by your actions on your journey.

Seek to discover these truths

It will propel you faster toward your dreams.

Faith

Anticipation is the road map to dreams

and the path clearer to make it happen.

Life

The nature of man is to walk on the path laid by their fathers

and to learn from them. Forge forward to new paths

that you alone discover.

Individuality is the birthright

for the next generation.

Life

The beauty in life is the breath of a new day

to change for the better.

Life

To live a life without regrets is chasing most of your dreams

till they are below you.

Faith

Forgiveness is given freely

The only price is acceptance

Regret

One of the true horrors in the human experience

Is would I have been a success if I tried?

<u>Warning</u>

If you accept failure you welcome defeat. For compromise

sees in gray not the black and white of good and evil.

There is no gray. If you are not walking toward good

you are walking backward to evil.

<u>Warning</u>

Fear creates its own sorrow

Just as faith forms its own pathway

<u>Truth</u>

Focus not on the road but the end of the journey

Warning

Temptation is a whisper that turns louder.

If you silence it with righteousness the soft voice

goes no further but in to deafness.

Faith

Practice confidence not failure for you will succeed

in one or the other by the measure of desire.

Action

To embrace failure is to accept the teachings of those

who are defeated by their own choices.

For we all teach lessons to others with our actions.

Warning

To see the color of the skin is to be colorblind to the beauty

of the heart and the spectral rainbow of the soul.

Warning

If you comment on life too much

you are dead to the experience of living it.

No comment.

Truth

True wealth is when it is earned not stolen

The only thing that you are allowed to steal

is that which is free

It is the perception and application of knowledge.

Horde it then share it for others to steal.

Truth

The worst teacher is the one who believes

he cannot learn from his students

and forgets when they were one.

Wisdom

The worst knowledge is the wisdom never applied

Warning

Once again the past can be whirlpools to engulf you

If you fight the currents you can be free

to sail the open seas of the future

Truth

Art is the self respect of passion to expression.

Wealth

True wealth is given from the heart before

the first dollar is thrown to charity.

Warning

If money is your god then the devil

is not having enough

Warning

A drowned flower dies in too much water.

An egotistical person dies in too much self praise.

One is watered by other hands

and the other being suffocated by their own voice.

Warning

One of the greatest treasures is respect.

Everyone needs it and will fight for it.

Great wars begin with this and always will.

Warning

A half truth is no truth at all just another lie

Truth

There is no love in criticism but there is love in explanation.

Warning

Anger is the acid that burns the bond between two hearts.

Warning

To whisper a lie is to scream out in jealousy

Warning

If the goal is unset your goal becomes to fail

Truth

Changing the course of a stream takes but one stick

As changing a life starts with one action in the chosen

direction

Regret

The shadows of the past will always be behind us

And the light of the future to move ahead is your guide

Give no power to regret

It is only a grey fog to dim the light of a new beginning

www.ingramcontent.com/pod-product-compliance
Lightning Source LLC
Chambersburg PA
CBHW070230290526

45789CB00004B/1558